PLAYS WITH WORDS

PLAYS WITH WORDS
FUN WITH HOMONYMS AND HOMOPHONES!

Bruce P. Attwood

PLAYS WITH WORDS
FUN WITH HOMONYMS AND HOMOPHONES!

iUniverse books may be ordered through booksellers or by contacting:

iUniverse
1663 Liberty Drive
Bloomington, IN 47403
www.iuniverse.com
1-800-Authors (1-800-288-4677)

ISBN: 978-1-5320-9232-9 (sc)
ISBN: 978-1-5320-9233-6 (e)

Library of Congress Control Number: 2020900402

Print information available on the last page.

iUniverse rev. date: 01/21/2020

After getting out of the army in 1980 and not finding employment in the communication equipment repair field, I fell into the job of being a drywaller; the hands do the work, and the brain is free to go gallivanting off! Almost forty years later, it was time to try new stuff: playing with words!

You need to come up with your homophones, figure out how to get them into a sentence, and then figure out how to build a story so you can use that sentence! Some simply will not work, like *peeked, peaked,* and *piqued*: they cannot be said consecutively with any sense, no matter how hard you try. I know these things!

And one-liners are many! However, sometimes you must build a story so you can use that one line because it will not stand alone. Coming up with a story line is where the fun is. My favorite one is done to a very familiar nursery rhyme song tied together to the first Billy Jack movie, but that is toward the rear of the book.

When that has been accomplished, it's time to share, and I do! It's stand-up comedy for everybody who happens to cross my path! I've also been in front of audiences five times, from Laughs in Totem Lake, Washington, to Tony V's in Everett, Washington.

All of these began as verbal stories and were done with a lot of different facial expressions, so changing from a verbal rendition to a written one is quite entertaining and exciting. This is what I have come up with. I hope you like it.

Bruce P. Attwood

Homonym: each of two or more words having the same spelling or pronunciation but different meanings and origins.

Homophone: each of two or more words having the same pronunciation but different meanings, origins, or spellings, Each of a set of symbols denotes the same sound or group of sounds.

Or, This group of words sounds like that group of words, but spelled differently.

With this in mind, I have a new word, Homophonial, which would be a new Sniglet!

Homophonial: a sentence using two or more homophones or phrasal homophones, each spelled differently and said consecutively, and it must make sense.

The following pages should serve as a dandy set of examples. Enjoy yourself!

Aroma International: it's a scratch-and-sniff company! Their most expensive product sells for $1,800. It smells really good and lasts a long time. Their cheapest one goes for only a penny. And they do deliveries!

Well, one day, this fellow walks in and makes his order. The clerk hands him his receipt and says, "Thanks! This is your receipt for your one cent scent sent!"

Bill and May have a Groovy Things mail order company. But it's a bit different because Bill will mail female stuff, and May'll mail male stuff!

The bald guy had a toupee to pay for!

And for some more creativity ...

That little germ, a flu bug! And his name was, believe it or not, Flu! Well, he was outdoors, and he so wanted to get into the house to get those people sick; it's his job, you know. The doors were locked, and the windows were shut tight, but there had to be a way in! He sat back to ponder for a few moments when it finally came to him! Aha! Up on the roof he went, and down the chimney flue flew Flu!

I love this language of ours; been playing with it for so many moons!

But wait! I can't leave out anyone!

The indigenous tribes of Washington State were going to get together and have a big powwow, light show, shindig—a great big party. But one tribe thought they'd pull a fast one and upstage the whole nine yards. When the light show happened, the lights came on, and yes, they did! But only on one tribe! They called it the Illumination of the Lummi Nation!

I love the way my mind thinks! Actually, *Lummi* rhymes with *rummy*! But that doesn't work so well!

You do it the one way, but Norma Lee normally does it another way.

The geologist: "I said I meant sediment!"

The cow told her calf, like all mothers do from time to time, "It's past your pasture time!"

Now we're getting primed for some more entertaining mixtures: using animals and names and such!

Remember—we have to come up with two or more words or phrases sounding the same, spelled differently, and said consecutively—and it needs to make sense! The entertainment continues …

That cat named Pa! How he got the name, I'm not really sure, but who cares? He was fast—lightning quick! He was so fast they had to do a documentary on him. They brought in the film crew and got a film of him going after a little bird. Then they had to bring in the narrator to narrate the film. And he started with, "Pa, he's creeping through the grass, left paw, right paw, left paw. Then, he hunkers down, moving forward … left paw, right paw, left paw. Then, Pa's paws pause." You don't even need to finish this story!

Word Usage 101—a touch of humor!

Now for a few more simple ones …

Her score was three to two; his score was three to two too!

Contemplated adding something about Gender Equality but my sister said, "No you don't!"

A cargo ship carries cargo, obviously, in three different areas usually: aft, the rear of the ship, holds five boxes; midship holds six boxes; and fore, for four more!

There was an immigrant from the Middle East—not sure from what country, but his name was Saud. He was an energetic, young sort looking for work, and he finally got a job with that small, grass-growing company! It was perfect for him … Saud sawed sod!

Some of the simple ones took the longest time to figure out how to say consecutively. Some use words that are said to not be used under any circumstances, like *thru*, but knowing that, it still really wants to work!

Like this one: They told him to crawl through, throw thru, and to continue. So, he crawled through, threw thru, and continued!

A lot of chortling on that one! Then one must be creative and think outside the box.

Some start out very educationally, like this one about our amphibian friends! And we get to meet Billy …

Frogs. They go through four phases, right? The egg, the tadpole, the pollywog, and then they become a frog, right? Okay, we have our little pond with bunches of frog eggs in it. The eggs go through their first phase, so now we have a pond full of little tadpoles, aye? Well, we have Sally, Mary, and Faye, three little girl tadpoles that are swimming around and doing little-girl-tadpole things, having fun. They start going through the next phase, to be the pollywog, when that mean kid Billy, he comes down and pours a bunch of nasty stuff into the water! Oh, don't be a Billy! Well, Sally and Mary, they went spiraling off, but it didn't faze Faye's phase!

And a couple more easy ones that kind of go together; you'll see ...

That dearest little girl, her name was Mary. The most cheerful sort, she was always happy and helping people everywhere, and soon she was called Merry Mary by most everyone! "Hi, Merry Mary," was heard all the time! Well, to make a long story short, Tommy, her best friend, announced that he was going to marry Merry Mary.

A simple story, and here's another along the same lines ...

That smart little fellow Barry! Entrepreneur unequaled! As in holy moly! He opened up a small fruit stand and called it Barry's Berries. Soon he was known all over as Berry Barry! He got a bunch of his school friends together and had them picking berries, paying them very well. He had berry sales almost unheard of, and to make a long story short, he died unexpectedly. They had to bury Berry Barry. A tragic loss indeed!

Can't leave Alaska out of this; It's where I grew up …

The Far North! Icebergs and glaciers—can't have one without the other, aye? In this one area, the ice floes come down out of the fjords and make their way out to sea. Usually, with there being so many, they have an annual contest to pick and see whose floes get to the outer markers first! Five bucks a berg or floe, the names are entered, and the contest starts. Every year, Florence tried her best, and she won two years ago. This year she bought two bergs and two floes, and she won! The headline: "Flo's Floes Flows Fastest!"

If you caught the misusage then you get an extra point! I knew it and the editor caught it too!

And then there are the reachers ... as in, "Really? Really?" But the creativity ...

The psychotic stairs! Bad news there: they only go up, and there's no way to get off! They put up some barricades and roped them off, with eleventeen signs saying the worst things to keep people away. "Bad things will happen if you get on the stairs! Stay off the stairs!" That kind of stuff.

Then one day, this girl hopped over all the defenses and stepped up on the first stair. "I'm staying right here!" she yelled. Well, it immediately drew a bunch of bystanders, and they yelled, "Get off the stairs!" She wouldn't listen and instead took another step up. "I am staying right here," she said with a wild look around. Then, in front of all the onlookers, she stopped and got this way faraway, vacant look. All went quiet, and they watched as she succumbed to the ... stair stayer stare!

It's not my fault! Good earthquake pun, there!

And then we have Santa Claus, and another silly scenario …

Worst-case scenario! An "Oh No! Mr. Bill" moment if there ever was one!

If, in the case of an emergency, the sleigh goes down, certain things may happen.

Sleigh is in the drift, reindeer are scattered about, no help is to be found, and poor Santa is getting hungry.

If worse comes to worst, and he can corral one of them reindeer, then he can administer the Santa Claus Claws Clause, and not be quite so hungry …

Oh no!

And then some really simple ones!

How did the butcher introduce his wife? Meet Patty!

And ones having nothing to do with much of anything …

If you have three flies in your kitchen, which one is the cowboy? The one on the range!

And which is the football player? He's in the Sugar Bowl!

Or the curtain rod Curt and Rod put up.

That goes well with the following:

What do you call two guys with no arms and no legs in a window? Curt and Rod.

Thinking further than one can reach …

If Bayer, the aspirin company, had a mascot, and it was a bear, and the bear was naked, we'd have a bare Bayer bear!

And now for another clever one!

What do you call a bummed-out guy in a submarine? A subdued sub dude!

This one is in honor of my dad. I needed an old guy to make it work! God rest his soul. This is one of my better verbal deliveries!

The wood carver, that old guy, got his first whittling knife when he was about seven. Eighty years later, with a warehouse full of carvings from too many moons carvin', he was still whittling away just for fun! Retired, he was working on this farm scene, working on the family of sheep, and having a good time! He picked up the baby sheep, the lamb if you will, made from alder. He likes to talk to 'em too! Well, he finished sanding the baby sheep, put it up on the shelf, and said, "Sit, you Alder lamb!" And it did! So, he picked up the next one, a male sheep—the ram, if you will, made out of oak. He finished sanding it, put it up on the shelf, and said, "Sit, you oak ram," and it did so quietly. He grabbed the last one, finished up the last bit of sanding, and with a silly grin, set it up on the shelf and said,"Sit, you yew ewe!"

Then we come across the one with four in a row. Very difficult! In fact, it's the only one so far! Here it is …

Out in the African Veldt, the Serengeti Plain if you will, there was a herd of gnus, a deerlike creature also known as a wildebeest! They were gallivanting around, having fun, and doing what gnus do, except for this young gnu. He was malcontent, wasn't happy, and didn't want to be there. He wanted to be with his uncle's herd across the way, and his uncle's name happened to be Noo, capital N, o, o! Noo the gnu!

Well, one morning, this young gnu woke up and he was Mr. Disgruntled. He said to himself, "I'm out of here," so off he went, skirting the hyena packs and the lion prides. He finally made it to his uncle's herd so now we can say, "The new Gnu knew Noo!"

More cleverness …

Mozart was such a smart little boy! He got himself a lawnmower and was going change it up. He was going to call it lawn graffiti! He would have the people bring out the art they didn't like and put it on their grass, so in reality, Mozart mows art!

They were having a hard time trying to figure out how get the colors just right, so they called in an expert. They decided to call Hugh, of Hugh's Hues!

Imagine: you're given two dice and told to go into a room. You do so, and it's full of all the games one can play with two dice. The most beautiful people are there and they all want to play with you. Could that not be called a "pair of dice" paradise?

Every once in a while, you can find one that works well with music, and I use this one to end my stand-up routine using the Billy Jack movie. I tell them, "Tonight I will leave a song in your head, and when you go to leave in your car, it will pop into it, and there is nothing you can do about it! Ready?"

The Toad

Before he went down the stream, they told the toad that he had to do it! He said, "I'm not going to doing it!"

Well, they said he had to!

He said, "I am *not* going to do it!"

They said, "Well, we're gonna make you!"

Well, he looked at 'em and said, "Go for it!"

So, they grabbed him, tied him, and pulled him up! Then, they put his toe on the line. So …

The towed toad toed the line before he went down the stream!

(That last line is sung to the music of "Row, Row, Row Your Boat.")

As an ending, or when leaving, some like to say, "I'm going to make like a tree and leave." No, no, no!

Use "I'm going to make like a purchasing agent!" They'll look at you funny, so you say, "What does a purchasing agent do? Purchases stuff!"

And another word for purchase? "Buy, er, bye!"

Or even better …

Make like a bargain hunter and "make a good buy."

And on that note, I hope you enjoyed my wit!

Bruce Attwood

Printed in the United States
By Bookmasters